dont
hunt
sharks

Ella
dunleavy

I love
aniamals

Pray
Every day
and
be
Kind ♥

Sophie Corrigan x

ANIMAL
BFFs

Frances Lincoln
Children's Books

Contents

Introduction	4
Animal BFFs	8

- - - - - - - - - - - - - -

Ostriches and zebras	10
Grey wolves and striped hyenas	14
Egrets and water buffaloes	18
Grouper fish and octopuses	22
Warthogs and banded mongooses	26
Oxpeckers and big mammals	30
Goby fish and pistol shrimp	34
Frogs and tarantulas	38
Capybaras and wattled jacanas	42

Remora fish and sharks	46
Sea anemones and hermit crabs	50
Elephants and baboons	54
Caimans and butterflies	58
Cleaner fish and ocean creatures	62
Coyotes and badgers	66
Crocodiles and plovers	70
Sloths and sloth moths	74
Marine iguanas and lava lizards	78
Anemones and clownfish	82

Sally Lightfoot crabs and sea lions	86	Atlantic puffins and rabbits	124
Deer and turkeys	90	Hoverflies and wasps	128
Squirrels and songbirds	94	Hermit crabs and sea snails	132
Friends from afar	98	Animal enemies	136
Scarlet king snakes and eastern coral snakes	100	Frogfish and small sea creatures	138
Golden jackals and tigers	104	Cuckoos and dunnocks	142
Burrowing owls and rattlesnakes	108	Ruby-throated hummingbirds and spiders	146
Bushveld lizards and oogpister beetles	112	Drongo birds and meerkats	150
Arctic foxes and caribou	116	Glossary	158
Beavers and frogs	120		

HELLO THERE, PAL!

Nice of you to stop by.

We were just talking about how FRIENDSHIP makes the world go around!

We all know that monkeys like to HANG OUT,

birds of a feather FLOCK together,

crocodiles often CHEW THE FAT with each other

and meerkats love nothing more than a GROUP HUG!

But did you know there are also MANY unlikely and hidden relationships between DIFFERENT animal species?

The animal kingdom is WEIRD and WONDERFUL! For example...

Egret birds sometimes hitch a ride on water buffaloes, alerting them to danger while cleaning their coats.

Pistol shrimp are the most chill landlords ever. They share their burrows with goby fish. In return, the goby alerts their almost-blind roommate to danger by poking them.

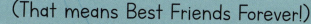

Plover birds climb inside crocodiles' mouths to clean their teeth! Now THAT is what I call trust.

Keep reading to find out WHY we are ANIMAL BFFs.

(That means Best Friends Forever!)

And also why some of us are ANIMAL ENEMIES, too!

There's some SERIOUS SCIENCE behind our relationships with each other!

Interaction between two different species is called SYMBIOSIS. There are three different types of SYMBIOTIC RELATIONSHIPS...

MUTUALISM

MUTUALISM is the friendliest type of symbiosis, and it means the friendship we have BENEFITS BOTH of us!

Think of it like 'I'll scratch your back and you'll scratch mine'.

COMMENSALISM

COMMENSALISM is when only ONE OF US gets something out of the relationship, and the other knows nothing about it.

Sort of like a secret admirer or a friend from afar.

That's the prettiest shell I've ever seen!

Why are you staring at me...?

PARASITISM

PARASITISM is the opposite of friendly! It is when ONE OF US benefits from the relationship, and the other LOSES OUT.

It might seem selfish, but everyone in the animal kingdom is just trying to survive... sometimes at any cost!

He gained our trust and stole our lunch!

Deal with it!

How rude!

Worst. Day. Ever.

Welcome to our friendship group.

We are <u>ANIMAL BEST FRIENDS FOREVER!</u>

In the following section, you'll hear from all sorts of MUTUAL animal friends. You'll find out why we are so close, what we do for each other and how our friendships bring so much to our lives.

OSTRICHES and ZEBRAS

Here I come, ready or not!

Now, where is Ostrich hiding...

Why is this game so difficult?

Seeking zebra

FIND US IN: SAVANNAHS, AFRICA

FRIENDLY FACTS:

* Zebras and ostriches graze together on the savannah for increased safety – both species benefit from the other's heightened senses so they can avoid danger (such as hungry lions!) by sensing it quickly.

* There's safety in numbers – both zebras and ostriches are herd animals, which means they stay together in large groups. The more individuals looking out for danger, the better!

* The pair can often be seen with wildebeest and gazelle, too, for the same safety reasons. Wildebeest are sometimes brave enough to fight lions while their friends run away.

* Zebras' ears are larger and rounder than horses' ears, and they can also turn in almost every direction. The ostrich, on the other hand, has the largest eye of any land mammal on Earth! Each eye measures 5 cm across, which is bigger than the ostrich's brain!

We like to graze and hang out together, relaxed because we've got each other's backs.

They say two eyes are better than one, but we think two eyes AND two ears are best!

GREY WOLVES and STRIPED HYENAS

Thanks for sharing your toys with me, Wolf! You're so kind.

Am I OK to keep this cool hat?

Cute party hat Wolf lent Hyena. Sharing is caring!

Hehehehehe!

FIND US IN: THE NEGEV DESERT, ISRAEL

Sneaky posture

Carcass-crushing chompers

FRIENDLY FACTS:

* Both the grey wolf and the striped hyena eat much of the same stuff. This includes hares, birds, lizards, snakes and larger prey like gazelle and farmers' livestock. Both species also like to snack on carrion (dead animals) and scavenged trash!

* Hyenas have an amazing sense of smell, which helps them to track down prey. They also have mega-strong jaws, the most powerful of any mammal, and this helps them to crush carcass bones – and crack open things like old cans of food.

* Despite having a worse sense of smell, wolves are better hunters than hyenas because they hunt in packs. They're also faster and more nimble.

* The predators have been spotted hunting together in the Negev desert in Israel, where only 29 mm of rain falls each YEAR! These extreme conditions might be the reason why the two BFFs hunt together. It's tough out there!

We DON'T actually work out together, but egrets DO keep a buffalo LOOKING GOOD!

Water buffaloes like me need our coats cleaned regularly from all those pesky, itchy bugs…

Annoying fly or tasty egret snack?

…and luckily we egrets LOVE to eat bugs so we're happy to do the job!

Bug-riddled buffalo coat

A ride on your back is a great way for us egrets to get around when we're feeling lazy.

FIND US IN: SOUTHEAST ASIA

FRIENDLY FACTS:

* Egrets sit on water buffaloes to eat insects in their shaggy coats, as well as flies that are attracted to the buffaloes. This relationship benefits both creatures — the water buffalo is cleaned of bugs and germs, and the egret gets a tasty snack!

* Egrets get the added bonus of eating any bugs that the buffalo shakes up in the grass as it forages — creatures in the grass have no choice but to move out of the buffalo's way, and the back of a buffalo is the perfect vantage point for an egret to spot them! Being carried to different water holes on a buffalo's back also saves the egret from expending energy looking for somewhere to hunt.

* The egret's beak is perfectly suited for harpooning the bugs and flies that are attracted to the buffalo's eyes. Luckily, they're very gentle when snacking so they don't have to worry about an angry buffalo!

You guys also keep an eye out for danger when I'm grazing! I'm really grateful for that.

All aboard the buffalo bus!

Bug-biting beak

Wetland wading (and occasionally lazy) legs

We DON'T exactly dance together...
but the way we HUNT together is well planned and choreographed beautifully!

It's annoying when I can't reach my supper. So I ask my octopus friend to help me out with his skinny tentacles.

Groovy grouper bod for dancing

Yep – my many tentacles are perfectly suited to wriggling about in the coral to scare out the fish.

Wriggly tentacle for poking around in small spaces

Like I always say, 'If you don't ASK, you don't GET!'

FIND US IN: CORAL REEFS, AUSTRALIA AND ASIA

Grouper Fish also tells me about prey I might have missed…

COMMUNICATION is the key to our successful relationship!

…and Octopus scares them out of hiding!

The way I ask for help is really cool – I turn my skin pale, which gets his attention, then stand on my head and wiggle my tail! Octopuses are super-smart, so they know what I'm trying to say right away.

This dance is our own amazing sign language!

FRIENDLY FACTS:

* Grouper fish and octopuses hunt the same types of small, fast fish that live and hide in the small crevices of coral reefs. Because the grouper fish are too big to follow the smaller fish into the crevices, they ask the octopuses to reach them using their tentacles.

* The communication between the grouper fish and octopus shows a high level of intelligence, maybe even rivalling chimpanzees. The dance is a type of underwater sign language!

* Groupers have other friends, too! They sometimes team up with moray eels for the same reason as the octopuses. They let the eels know that it's time to hunt with a different dance. The grouper forcefully shakes its head close to the eel's own head and raises its dorsal fin.

WARTHOGS and BANDED MONGOOSES

Thanks for giving me a makeover!

I am so lucky to have friends like you.

Best friend brushin'

Don't mention it!

Trendy trotter polish

Pink is SO your colour.

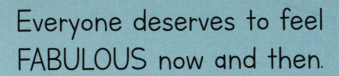

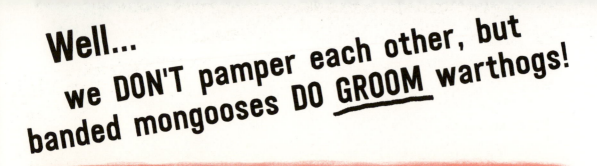

Well...
we DON'T pamper each other, but banded mongooses DO <u>GROOM</u> warthogs!

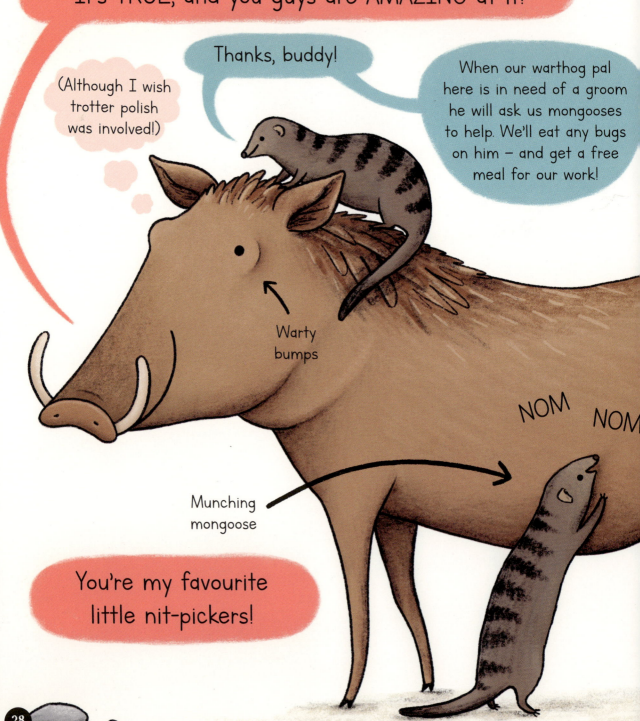

It's TRUE, and you guys are AMAZING at it!

Thanks, buddy!

(Although I wish trotter polish was involved!)

When our warthog pal here is in need of a groom he will ask us mongooses to help. We'll eat any bugs on him – and get a free meal for our work!

Warty bumps

NOM NOM

Munching mongoose

You're my favourite little nit-pickers!

FIND US IN: QUEEN ELIZABETH NATIONAL PARK, UGANDA

FRIENDLY FACTS:

* Warthogs are a type of wild pig, named for the warty bumps on their faces.

* Banded mongooses are small cat-like carnivores. Unlike other species of mongoose, who live solitary lives, banded mongooses live in family groups of up to 40 individuals! They love small insects – so much that they like to make their homes in termite mounds!

* Warthogs actively seek out banded mongooses to eat the ticks and other unwanted insects from their hair. This is an indicator of high intelligence, something that pigs are known to have.

* Mutualistic relationships between mammal species, like warthogs and banded mongooses, are very rare. It's a really special friendship!

Oxpeckers DO <u>HANG AROUND</u> animals on the savannah...

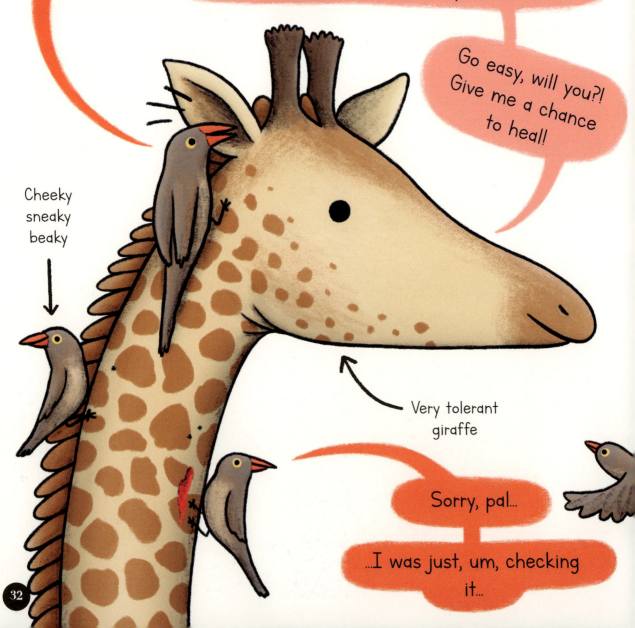

FIND US IN: SAVANNAHS, AFRICA

Some may say I don't deserve my SUPER BFF rosette, because my main diet is... BLOOD! What's a bit of blood between friends?

FRIENDLY (AND FIENDISH!) FACTS:

* Oxpeckers benefit a lot from their relationship with animals on the savannah. The larger animals give them an easy meal – the oxpeckers eat their host's ticks, bugs, dead skin and even earwax!

* Scientists always thought that this relationship was an example of mutualism. After all, the oxpeckers get a meal and the larger animals are cleaned from parasites.

* Now we know that the parasites are both the oxpeckers AND the ticks! The oxpeckers feast on the ticks for one reason – their BLOOD. The oxpeckers love blood so much that they have another source – the hosts themselves. They actively make sure that their wounds stay open for a steady supply. YUCK!

* Oxpeckers are perfectly suited to live in this way. Their flattened beaks can comb through the animal's hair (which they even use to build their nests!). They also have sharp claws that can easily cling to the back of a slippery hippo.

We DON'T garden together, but we DO SHARE a lovely HOME!

We live in domestic BLISS!

Shrimps like me are great at digging burrows to live in, but we're not so great at spotting danger because of our poor eyesight. So I invite Goby Fish to live with me and she looks out for danger! She has brilliant eyesight, after all.

I pay my shrimp pal 'rent' by alerting him to any trouble by wiggling my tail. He places one of his antennae on me so he can feel those movements!

FRIENDLY FACTS:

* The goby fish uses the pistol shrimp's burrow to protect itself from predators, and in return will watch out for danger for them both.

* The shrimp places an antenna on the goby while it's pottering around outside the burrow. This lets it know if the goby's tail is flicking, which is the predator alert!

* The shrimp only leaves the region of the burrow in daylight and accompanied by the goby.

* Whereas some burrows contain one shrimp and one goby, more often a burrow will contain several of each species.

* The burrow can be quite large – as deep as 60 cm into the ground – and divided into separate chambers.

FIND US IN: SOUTHERN AFRICAN WATERS

Googly goby danger-spotters

It's the perfect living arrangement.

Cosy burrow home

Tidy garden

Reassuring antennae touch

I actually do a little gardening outside our burrow when I can, despite my bad eyesight.

I like to keep the entrance tidy by clearing it of gravel, and I also nibble on the algae that grows nearby.

Ahh, there's no place like home!

37

FIND US IN: THE AMAZON RAINFOREST, SOUTH AMERICA

It's true, I'd never eat my froggy friend. Frog eats the ants that go after my eggs... and I've heard that she would taste awful!

Yes, the ant snacks are a bonus. I'm also WAY less likely to be eaten by a snake with big Tarantula as my bodyguard!

Pesky egg-eating ants

Um... guys? Let's NOT eat spider eggs today...

FRIENDLY FACTS:

* The Colombian lesserblack tarantula and the dotted humming frog both benefit from their relationship. The dotted humming frog gets protection from predators, and it eats small insects that are attracted to the tarantula's leftovers and eggs.

* The Colombian lesserblack tarantula can't protect its eggs alone. The ants are too small for the spider to catch!

* This mutualistic relationship is particularly interesting because small frogs are usually part of a large spider's diet.

* Sometimes the tarantula accidentally grabs its 'partner' frog thinking that it is prey. It examines the frog, and releases it once it recognises its special chemical signals!

41

We DON'T take selfies together, but capybaras ARE social butterflies. We're very <u>POPULAR</u> with other animals, especially jacana birds!

He is everyone's best pal.

Not only is he the world's comfiest perch, but we love him because he lets us eat bugs in his fur! Yummy.

Yep! Sometimes it hurts a bit, but I'm OK with it. I know it's for my own good really.

High-up eyes and nose

Webbed toes for swimming

SUPER BFF!

FIND US IN: SWAMPLANDS, SOUTH AMERICA

I'm so chilled-out that I'm happy to let almost any animal sit with me – or ON me!

Plucking 'n' preening

FRIENDLY FACTS:

* Capybaras are the world's LARGEST (and friendliest) rodents! Despite being cute, capybaras do something totally GROSS – they eat their own poop! This is called corpophagy. Capybaras eat grass that is difficult to digest, so they have to eat it AGAIN as poop. This helps them absorb more nutrients. Disgusting, but it works!

* Jacanas (and other birds) use capybaras as perches to travel around and to spot food from. The birds also groom them, and eat any bugs and ticks hiding in their hair and on their skin. Capybaras will often roll over to give them easier access to their tummies! It's a free meal for the birds, and a lovely spa treatment for the capybaras!

Huge feet for wading in the wetlands

They call me 'Nature's Armchair'.

45

We really DO STICK TOGETHER!

Remoras love being around sharks so much that we ATTACH ourselves to them!

Built-in suction cup

We have special dorsal fins on our heads that act just like suction cups! They let us cling onto our pal and travel around the ocean without using much energy.

Yeah, and you sometimes eat my leftovers and parasites and loose bits of skin too, don't you?

We do, yeah.

It's a bit gross, Remoras, but I'm here for it.

FIND US IN: WARM OCEANS, WORLDWIDE

We clean inside your mouth too, so cheers for not eating us (most of the time)!

We're so clingy – we've been known to latch onto rays, turtles, whales and even the occasional scuba diver!

As a general rule, if it's bigger than us and moving around, we want to get attached!

FRIENDLY FACTS:

* Remoras get a lot out of their relationship with a shark – free and easy transportation, food and protection from a top ocean predator! Sharks benefit from the relationship, too. Remoras keep their skin free from parasites, and the water around the shark clear of food scraps, which can turn into unhealthy organisms.

* Remora fish are sometimes known as suckerfish because of their sucker-like front dorsal fins.

* Sharks do sometimes find their friends a little TOO clingy – sandbar and lemon sharks have been known to SNACK on their remora pals! Well that's gratitude for you!

SEA ANEMONES and HERMIT CRABS

The wiggliest and giggliest of anemones

Piggyback rides are the BEST!

Sturdy shell

Careful carrying

Agreed — but you do know I'm a crab and not a pig, right?

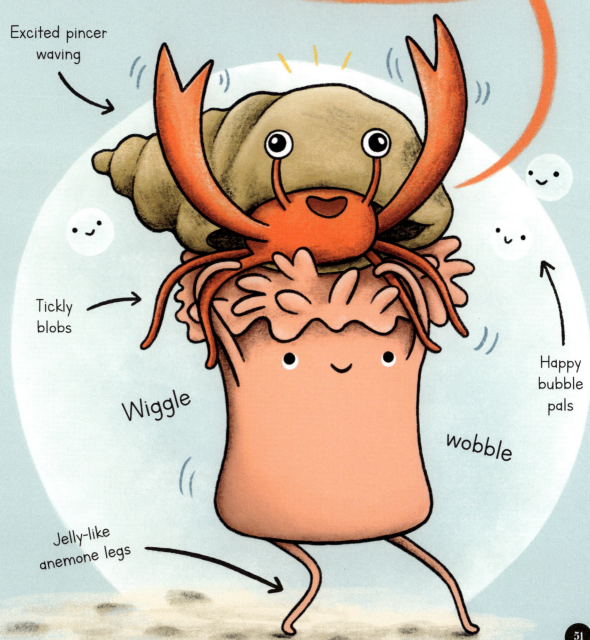

Well, we DON'T give each other piggybacks, but sea anemones DO HITCH A RIDE on hermit crab shells!

And it's a positive thing for BOTH of us!

FRIENDLY FACTS:

* Hermit crabs and sea anemones share a really fascinating (and unusual!) relationship. The sea anemone does a great job at protecting the hermit crab from predators. Scientists aren't sure how they communicate, but when the crab alerts the anemone to danger, the anemone extends its stinging tentacles. Predators are less likely to eat a hermit crab if it has a dangerous-looking anemone on its back!

* In return for this life-saving protection, the hermit crab provides easy meals for its anemone pal. The anemone will gladly eat any leftovers the crab leaves.

* Anemones can't really move around much if they're not latched onto a hermit crab shell, so their relationship gives the anemone the added bonus of transport.

* Hermit crabs and sea anemones can stay together for life! Even when the crab outgrows its shell and has to find a larger one, it will take the anemone along. They also grow bigger together at about the same rate. Now that really IS friendship!

FIND US IN: INDO-PACIFIC WATERS

I have fantastically wiggly tentacles that will ZAP any predator...

...making me one of the ocean's cutest little bodyguards.

You really do protect me! You're the best jiggly friend ever.

I sort of offer a 'Meals on Wheels' service to Anemone – it's the least I could do as they've SAVED MY LIFE on multiple occasions!

Sneaky stinging tentacles to ward off predators

Sticky underside to latch onto the shell

Second-hand sea snail shell

Don't mention it, buddy. Now get a move on, I'm hungry!

OK, friendship bracelets AREN'T involved... but baboons DO something MORE IMPORTANT for elephants!

We LOOK OUT for them – literally!

We sit in treetops and look out for danger, alerting our friends when we see a predator – like a lion.

In return for this, we keep the baboons' thirsts quenched by digging water holes with our mighty tusks!

Strong soil-scraping tusks

FIND US IN: SAVANNAHS, AFRICA

It's important to stay hydrated because it's VERY hot where we live, and water can be hard to find.

Savannah scanners

Tree-climbing limbs

FRIENDLY FACTS:

* Groups of baboons (or 'troops') follow elephant herds around when they're thirsty, because elephants dig water holes in the soil with their tusks. They happily drink alongside each other – friends who hydrate together stay together!

* In return for the drink, baboons operate a warning system from the treetops. Even if they're high enough to be safe themselves, they howl or shriek when they see danger, which gives the elephants time to escape.

* Elephants are the largest land mammals, but there are LOTS of dangerous predators that could target a baby elephant. And poachers can target adult elephants, too. Thank goodness the baboons have their buddies' backs.

FIND US IN: THE AMAZON RAINFOREST, SOUTH AMERICA

FRIENDLY FACTS:

* Butterflies feed on caiman tears because they contain micronutrients and sodium (salt). This is known as lachryphagy.

* The main diet of the butterfly is nectar, which is very sugary and doesn't have much sodium in it. But the butterflies need sodium in their diet to keep a good metabolism and to produce their little butterfly eggs – so caiman tears are perfect for a healthy drink!

* Caimans aren't harmed by the butterflies and can sit for long periods of time while the butterflies have a drink. It's currently unknown if the caimans benefit from the relationship – apart from looking good! This means that the relationship could be commensalistic rather than mutualistic.

You're so pretty, and you make me feel SPECIAL! Plus, you're gentle with my eyes, and watching you flutter around is so relaxing.

We love you too!

FIND US IN: SHALLOW WATERS, WORLDWIDE

Ahhh, there's nothing like stopping by a cleaning station for a pamper! You are SUCH professionals.

Glad you think so because your dead skin is mega-tasty. Please drop by again soon!

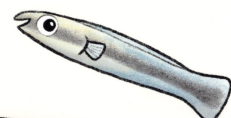

FRIENDLY FACTS:

* 'Cleaner fish' is a name for many species of fish that specialise in providing a cleaning service to other sea creatures. They eat dead skin, parasites and infected tissue from their 'clients' or 'hosts'.

* The client – which could be anything from a sea turtle to a manta ray – actively seeks out the cleaner fish's 'cleaning station' to keep themselves in tip-top condition! The cleaners are vital to the health of many sea creatures, so luckily the clients choose not to eat them!

* Cleaner fish can recognise familiar clients, and vice versa. Both parties are careful to be on their best behaviour with each other to keep their mutual relationship strong – the less the cleaners bite their clients, and the less the clients chase their cleaners, the better chance they have of staying BFFs!

* It's a win-win situation, as the ocean creatures get a free pamper and clean, and the cleaner fish gets an easy meal.

Coyotes and badgers DON'T sunbathe together... but we DO <u>HUNT</u> together!

We are GREAT at teamwork. We use each other's strengths to catch our dinner, and we look super-cool doing it, too.

But that DID look really relaxing...

Den digger with cool claws

We get on so well that coyotes prefer to hunt with badgers than with other coyotes! He's my brother from another mother – I just love him.

Same here, mate – hunting with a cool coyote is the best. Another badger would get in my way while I'm digging! Plus your brilliant eyesight is mega-helpful for spotting prey that I might miss.

FIND US IN: GRASSLANDS, NORTH AMERICA

Those eyes... and claws... we don't stand a chance, do we?

Shh! Get back inside!

Prairie prowler with exceptional eyesight

FRIENDLY FACTS:

* Despite the fact that badgers and coyotes compete for prey, their different hunting techniques mean that teaming up is logical. Badgers can smell prey hiding in a burrow, while coyotes can spy prey above ground. Their partnership is so successful that they can catch a third more food together compared with going it alone.

* The badger chases the prey underground so that it runs out of its burrow – right towards the coyote, waiting to pounce on it outside! Sometimes they swap roles – the coyote scares the prey into its burrow. Then the badger can use its claws to burrow down after it.

* The team hunts in open prairie lands, with few places to hide. The land makes it difficult to stalk prey sneakily – which is why they have to be speedy and smart!

* Working together helps both of the animals to save energy. Their prey (mice, groundhogs, prairie dogs and ground squirrels) moves fast, so it makes sense for the predators to share the workload to prevent themselves getting tired.

We DON'T eat sugary snacks together... but plovers DO CARE FOR crocodile TEETH!

No toothbrush required →

FRIENDLY FACTS:

* When a crocodile sits with its mouth open, it's giving a signal to an Egyptian plover bird to come and clean its teeth!

* The plover fearlessly climbs inside the crocodile's mouth (eek!) and picks at the leftovers in between the croc's teeth and gums with its long pointed beak.

* Removing old food keeps the crocodile's mouth free from parasites and debris. Just like brushing your teeth! Meanwhile, the plover gets a snack.

* Crocodiles don't tend to eat plover birds (although they easily could). They recognise that dental hygiene is more important than a small feathery meal!

The pyjamas are a little far-fetched... but sloths and sloth moths DO <u>HANG OUT</u> all the time!

We actually LIVE in our sloth friend's fur, EAT the algae growing on his back and lay our EGGS in his POOP! We just couldn't do without him.

Call me a walking ecosystem!

I like giving my moth mates a piggyback – the more the merrier! I need them just as much as they need me.

They help algae grow on my fur, which is a weird style choice, but I LOVE it. The algae helps to camouflage me from predators, and it's nutritious. Always eat your greens!

We agree. Sloth fur algae is the tastiest stuff around, and it keeps us hidden from predators. We love you, Slothy!

Edible algae

76

FIND US IN: CENTRAL AND SOUTH AMERICA

FRIENDLY FACTS:

* Sloth moths have evolved to call a sloth 'home sweet home'. They live exclusively in the fur of a sloth.

* The three-toed sloth climbs down from its tree-top home just once a week to poop. Then the sloth moth lays its eggs in the dung!

* Sloth moths benefit from the relationship by having a safe refuge from predators (a cosy sloth-fur-home), easy access to food (they eat sloth sweat as well as algae) and a safe place to raise young (sloth poop, which their larvae eat).

* The moths help out the sloths, too. They provide nutrients that encourage algae growth. The algae is both camouflage and food for the sloth.

* A single three-toed sloth has been recorded with over 120 sloth moths in its fur. Now that's a BIG sleepover!

Weekly poop/sloth moth nursery

Lay your eggs in me, Mothies!

MARINE IGUANAS and LAVA LIZARDS

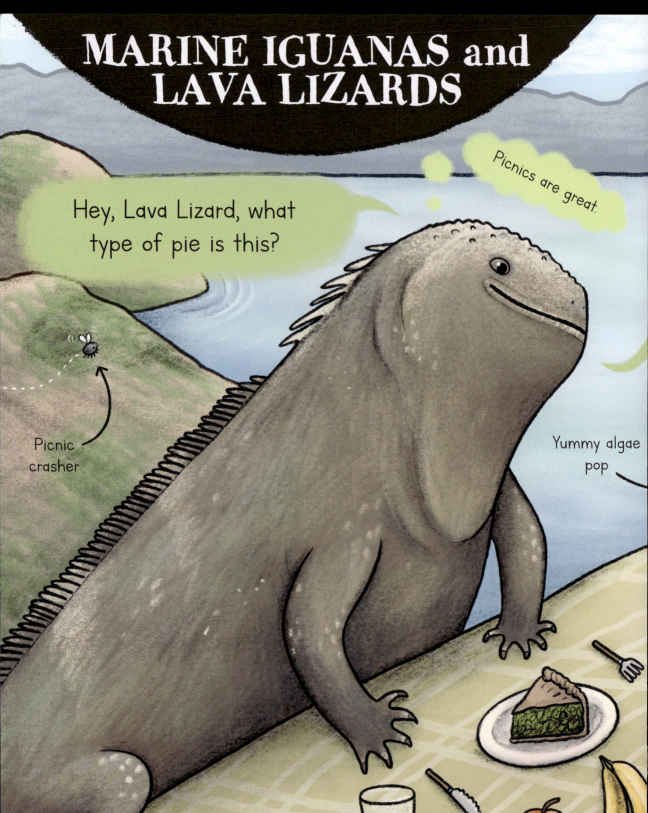

78

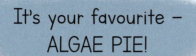

Well, we DON'T share picnics...

...but I DO rely on Lava Lizard's HUNGER to help me out!

It's true! I eat the annoying flies that buzz around you, and you're a herbivore who won't eat meat of any kind.

FRIENDLY FACTS:

* Lava lizards get an easy meal from this mutualistic relationship – they eat the flies that are attracted to sunbathing marine iguanas.

* Having flies buzzing around your head isn't much fun! Because the iguanas are algae-eating herbivores, they rely on the smaller carnivorous lizards to eat the annoying flies for them.

* When they're not eating flies, lava lizards also like to eat the marine iguanas' dead skin. Gross!

* It is believed that the marine iguanas evolved from land iguanas 10.5 million years ago, after a shared relative probably arrived at the Galápagos Islands on a raft of vegetation.

* On one Galápagos island there is a type of marine iguana that is sometimes called the Christmas iguana, because of its red and green colouring. You can also see the males fighting one another in December, as this is the mating season. Hardly in the Christmas spirit!

OK, we DON'T share a loving embrace... but we DO have a special relationship based on <u>TOUCH!</u>

My pal the clownfish is the ONLY fish that doesn't get stung by my lethal stinging tentacles.

Lucky me! It means I get to LIVE in the anemone. It's a wiggly fortress that protects only me!

FRIENDLY FACTS:

* Sea anemones live anchored to the sea floor and use their stinging tentacles (or 'nematocysts') to attract prey.

* Clownfish have developed an immunity to anemone toxins by performing a special 'dance'! The clownfish carefully touches the tentacles of the anemone with different parts of its body, and the fish develops a protective mucus layer which protects it from being stung.

* Once a clownfish has immunity to its own special anemone, that anemone is called its 'host', and the clownfish lives among it for the rest of its life. It's a forever home, and the clownfish actually can't survive without it.

* Clownfish are known for being quite aggressive. They are protective over their host anemone. Anemones return the favour by stinging anything that dares to come close to the pair.

* Clownfish are omnivores, and along with preening (or cleaning) the anemone of parasites, they seek out food such as zooplankton, worms, crustaceans and algae, but won't venture far from their host anemone. The anemone gets to eat the clownfish's leftovers!

FIND US IN: CORAL REEFS, AUSTRALIA AND ASIA

Clownfish is my personal preener and food deliverer, which is lovely. He also protects me, with his angry clowning around!

Not to be dramatic, but I cannot live without my Anemone.

Stinging tentacles

Bold colouring like a clown's face paint

It's you and me against the world, buddy!

We might NOT build sandcastles or eat ice cream, but we DO HANG OUT on the beach together!

I like nothing better than a chilled-out doze in the sun, but I do struggle a bit with ticks sometimes...

...that's where we step in!

We love to scurry about on Sea Lion's back, plucking away ticks with our pincers and keeping him free from parasites!

Luckily, we find these parasites TASTY! What can we say? It's an easy meal...

Snack spotters

Picky pincers

FIND US IN: THE GALÁPAGOS ISLANDS, SOUTH AMERICA

FRIENDLY FACTS:

* While relaxing by the water, sea lions allow crabs to remove any harmful parasites and debris from their fur. This is an easy meal for the crab!

* Both species are perfectly adapted to live on the shoreline. Sea lions can hold their breath for 20 minutes while fishing for their dinner, and the crabs use their pointed legs to grip onto rocks. They can even stay attached when being buffeted by a powerful wave!

* Sally Lightfoot crabs also share a similar relationship with marine iguanas, cleaning parasites from them and getting a meal in return.

* It is rumoured that Sally Lightfoot crabs were named after a Caribbean dancer. It's a fitting story, because the crabs are brightly coloured and agile. They can run very fast and even leap to get away from predators!

Beach body

FIND US IN: FORESTED AREAS, NORTH AMERICA

We have each other's backs, too. Turkey's eyesight is great, so he can spot and warn me of any danger nearby.

Deer's also on high alert! She uses smell to sense danger. Together, we're a lot safer!

Plus, we like the same food, which helps.

More acorns, Deer?

Yes, please!

Tasty acorns

FRIENDLY FACTS:

* White-tailed deer and turkeys are often seen grazing and interacting with each other in meadows and coniferous forests from southern Canada to South America.

* Their youngsters have also been seen playing together! They mostly play chasing games. How cute!

* Sadly, both species are targeted by human hunters, so they team up to protect each other. The deer uses its brilliant sense of smell and the turkey uses its excellent eyesight to gain the advantage. Together, the pair sense the hunters a lot quicker, which gives them a chance to get away.

* The turkey's vision is superb – three times as good as human vision. In the daytime, a turkey can see in colour, and, thanks to its neck, in almost 360 degrees.

FIND US IN: WOODED AREAS, WORLDWIDE

Because we have this agreement, you'll often see us co-existing and sharing food on bird tables and at feeders.

We miss NOTHING!

FRIENDLY FACTS:

* Squirrels are very aware of their surroundings. They can sense the tiniest changes in movements, sounds and smells.

* Birds rely on squirrel warnings, as they are very vulnerable to predators when they're foraging on the ground.

* In return, birds have incredible eyesight and can spot winged predators like hawks from long distances. Both species are at risk from these predators, so the squirrels pay close attention to the birds' movements and alarm calls.

* They both live in the trees (squirrels' nests are made out of leaves!), and have been known to use each other's nests when the other doesn't use it anymore. How sweet!

Ooh-be-do! I wanna be just like you...

We are FRIENDS FROM AFAR!

In this next section, we'll tell you about those of us that appreciate someone else, but without them really knowing about it. Kind of like how a famous person might INSPIRE you and change your life for the better, but they're CLUELESS about the good they've done.

Some of us animals are inspired enough to COPY other animals. Like where they live, what they sound like or what they look like! Basically, these next relationships are all examples of COMMENSALISM.

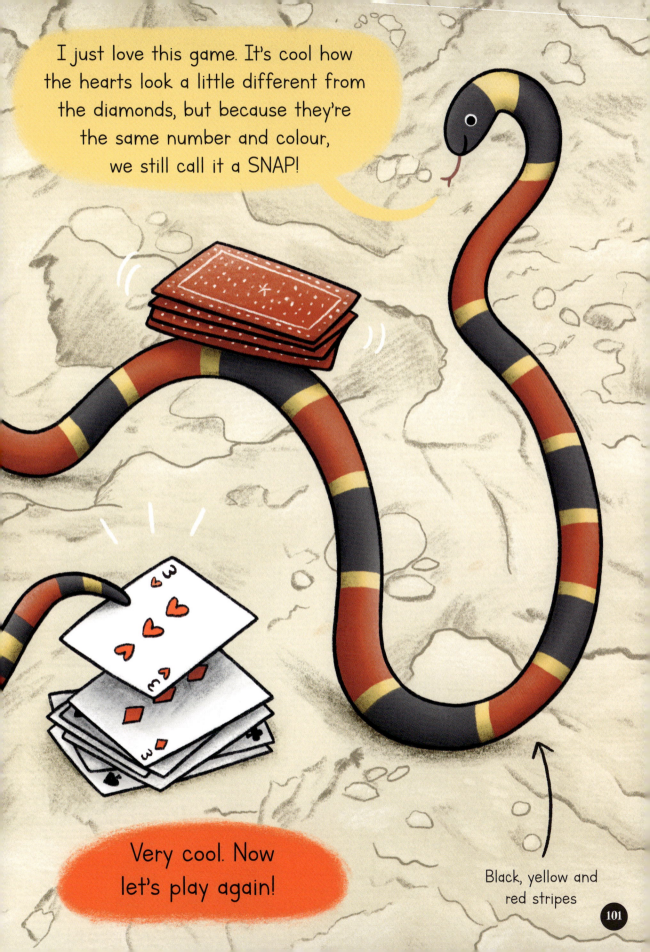

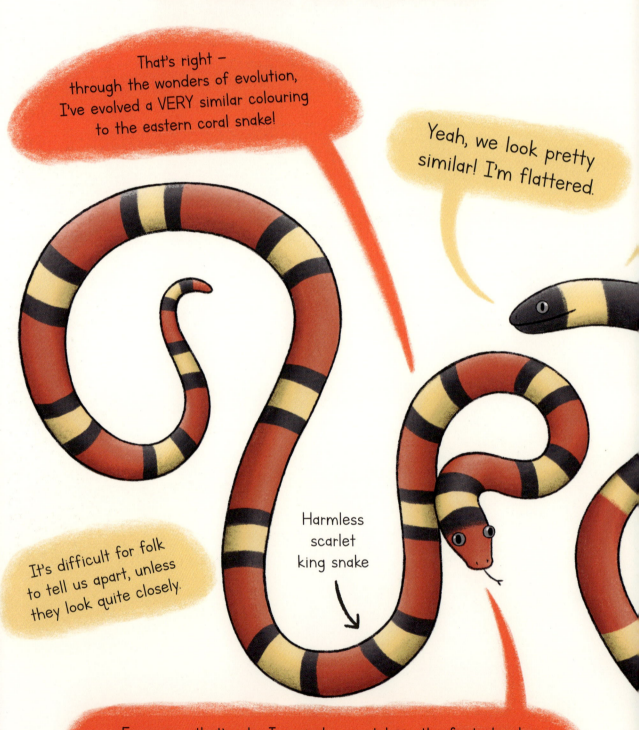

FIND US IN: SOUTH-EASTERN USA, NORTH AMERICA

GENIUS!

FASCINATING FACTS:

*   Eastern coral snakes kill with venom, whereas scarlet king snakes constrict their prey. This means that they squeeze their prey until the prey's blood can't reach its brain and it dies. King snakes eat rodents, birds, lizards, eggs – and sometimes other snakes!

*   The king snake is harmless to large predators and humans, so it imitates the colouring of the deadly coral snake to deter them. This type of imitation is called Batesian mimicry.

*   The pattern on the scarlet king snake isn't EXACTLY the same as that on the eastern coral snake, but it's close enough! The trick still works to keep its enemies away, so the king snake is free to slither another day.

*   There's even a rhyme to help you remember which snake is the harmless one!

Deadly eastern coral snake

'Red touches yellow, could kill a fellow.'

'Red touches black, a friend to Jack!'

FIND US IN: FORESTED AREAS, ASIA

Under-appreciated jackal

That's gratitude for you.

Pitiful leftover

FASCINATING FACTS:

* The relationship between golden jackals and tigers is an unusual one, because it's between a canine and a feline.

* Lone golden jackals follow lone tigers around, occasionally alerting their 'friend' to the presence of prey.

* The tiger tolerates the jackal – as long as it doesn't get too close! When the tiger finishes eating its prey, it allows the jackal to eat any leftovers – if there are any!

* Their unique relationship is best described as commensalism, because the tiger provides the jackal with a meal. Even if sometimes the jackal does alerts the tiger to a potential kill, the tiger doesn't need this interference to hunt. Mostly the tiger ignores the jackal.

Rattlesnakes AREN'T talented singers...

but burrowing owls DO <u>COPY</u> the <u>NOISES</u> they make!

FASCINATING FACTS:

* Burrowing owls and rattlesnakes are another example of Batesian mimicry. The owl scares predators away by pretending to be a rattlesnake.

* The owl does this by copying the rattlesnake's unique vocal hiss. The rattlesnake is unaffected by this.

* Despite their name, burrowing owls don't burrow, but instead live in burrows dug out by other animals, such as prairie dogs. Rattlesnakes also live in burrows, and they eat much of the same type of prey as the owls.

* Because of where they live, both species are vulnerable to predators, so using a rattle sound to ward them off is vital for both species' safety.

I shake my tail to make a THREATENING sound!

Everyone knows to run when they hear my tail rattling... that's why I'm called a rattlesnake!

← Dangerous rattlesnake

Just remember to keep your head up and walk in a straight line.
You're a natural on the catwalk!

You're such a good teacher.

Beetle beret

Trendy waistcoat

Beautiful beetle booties

You're a good student!

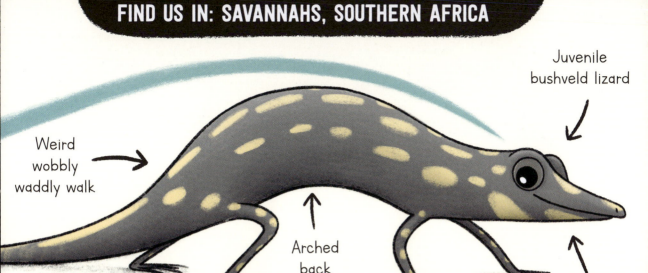

FASCINATING FACTS:

* The bushveld lizard uses Batesian mimicry to copy the colouration and walking style of the oogpister beetle. The oogpister is unaffected, but the lizard is protected from predators by using this trick.

* When threatened, the oogpister beetle walks in a jerky style, raises its abdomen, and sprays formic acid. The acid can cause temporary blindness, so predators know to keep their distance when the beetle is in this stance. 'Oogpister' actually means 'eye-spitter' in Afrikaans. YUCK!

* The tiny juvenile bushveld lizard starts its life the same colour as the oogpister, and adopts its stance and style of walking. Predators mistake the harmless lizard for the spitting beetle, and stay away.

* When they mature, bushveld lizards lose their spots and the oogpister beetle's distinctive walk because they're less at risk from being eaten.

ARCTIC FOXES and CARIBOU

FIND US IN: TUNDRAS, THE ARCTIC

FASCINATING FACTS:

* Arctic foxes and caribou live in the Arctic – one of the hardest places to live on Earth! Food is hard to find in this cold climate, so caribou have to shift piles of snow with their hooves to get to the lichens and fungi that grow beneath it.

* This helps the Arctic fox, which likes to eat small subnivean mammals. The caribou's digging scares the mammals up to the surface where the fox can catch them.

* This isn't the only way the Arctic fox can eat over winter. The fox also stores food, like bird eggs, in the permafrost during summer. This source of food can keep well for an entire year!

* Caribou make one of the longest mammal migrations on the planet! Every summer, they head north on a mammoth journey of 970 km. Some herds have been known to trudge up to 3200 km per year!

Hungry fox

How dare you! Can't a shrew get some peace and quiet around here?

FIND US IN: RIVERS AND LAKES, NORTH AMERICA

FASCINATING FACTS:

* Beavers are construction workers and do a lot to change the natural environment!

* Beavers dam flowing streams with pieces of wood they collect. This wood blocks the water flow to create a pond. When the pond is ready, the beavers then build a lodge that they can live in out of sticks, grasses and mud. Home sweet home!

* Frogs benefit from these ponds, and the areas close by, as the water flow is less turbulent so it is safer for them to lay their eggs in. Young frogs also benefit from the safety that still ponds provide.

* Beavers are the mermaids of the animal world! They can stay underwater for 15 minutes, and they also have a special set of transparent eyelids that allows them to see underwater. Sort of like goggles!

Beaver gets a special Friend from Afar Gold Star because, without realising it, building dams brings so many benefits to a bunch of OTHER species too, and it is mostly GREAT for the environment!

Puffins DON'T try to become flatmates with rabbits... but they DO <u>LIVE</u> in their <u>BURROWS!</u>

It's true! Rabbit's burrow is perfect for me to nest in. I just had to wait until it was empty before I moved myself in.

Fine by me, pal. I've already moved home anyway!

FASCINATING FACTS:

* Puffins move into and use cliffside rabbit burrows as a place to build their nests. They COULD dig out their own holes, but it's easier for them to use an abandoned rabbit burrow!

* Puffins mate for life, and they return to the same burrow for four months every year. Their chicks are called pufflings – how CUTE!

* Their relationship could also be described as PARASITIC! Occasionally, puffins will have the nerve to kick a rabbit out of its burrow, which isn't very nice at all! And in some parts of the world, like Iceland, it's the RABBITS that colonise the PUFFINS' nests. Puffins are very important to the Icelandic people, and it's no good that the non-native rabbits are disrupting the sea birds' breeding habits.

FIND US IN: ICELAND, GREENLAND, CANADA AND NORTHERN SCOTLAND

Oh, had you? I didn't really consider that you might still live here... that's good then! Thanks for making the place so COSY!

Don't mention it! See you around, neighbour.

Burrow-digging paws

Tonight's fish supper

127

Hoverflies DO get fashion tips from wasps... in a way... because they COPY their iconic yellow STRIPES!

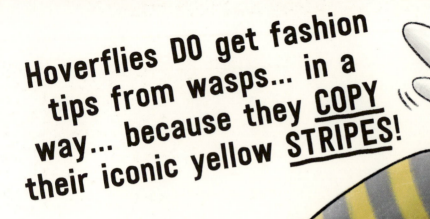

Wasp sting

I like to think of it as a high-visibility jacket! It's for my own safety, after all.

If I get mistaken for a wasp, predators think I can STING them, so they keep away from me!

Between you and me, I don't have a stinger, so I couldn't hurt a fly.

FIND US IN: GARDENS AND MEADOWS, WORLDWIDE

You're my harmless twin – and you've found a really CLEVER way to keep safe!

Stinger-less abdomen

FASCINATING FACTS:

* Hoverflies use Batesian mimicry to copy the colouring of wasps and bees for protection. The hoverfly benefits, while the wasp is unaffected.

* Despite looking similar, hoverflies (sometimes called flower flies) and wasps are from entirely different orders in the animal kingdom!

* Wasps are slightly bigger, have two more wings than hoverflies, and have smaller eyes. Hoverflies have bigger eyes and like to hover in one spot!

* Unlike wasps that can sting, hoverflies are completely harmless. Instead of using a sting for defence, they copy the look of the wasp so that predators just THINK they can sting them, and stay away!

* Both species are very beneficial to their ecosystems. They pollinate flowers and plants in gardens, and keep down the pesky aphid population.

Thank you both for being Flower Friends, too!

Hermit crabs DON'T draw pictures with sea snails...

but they DO MOVE INTO their SHELLS!

But only when the snail no longer needs it.
Rest in peace, buddy!

My time had come, I guess!

You can take comfort in the fact that your shell home has been recycled and reused – by me!

Oh, that's great.
I'm glad it's not gone to waste.
Gorgeous little shell, that is!

Second-hand shell

FIND US ON: SEASHORES, WORLDWIDE

I agree! And I'm so happy in my new home. You've left a wonderful legacy!

Ahh, that's lovely!

Dearly departed sea snail

FASCINATING FACTS:

* Hermit crabs are not true crabs, because they don't have hard exoskeletons or the ability to grow their own shells! They are extremely vulnerable because their bodies are soft. So hermit crabs use the discarded shells of dead sea snails for protection.

* When a sea snail dies, it leaves its hard shell on the seabed. Then a hermit crab finds the shell, tucks itself inside and carries it around on its back!

* As they grow, hermit crabs have to keep trading up their shells for bigger ones. The shell needs to be big enough for them to hide in.

* When a big snail shell is found, hermit crabs have been seen lining up in size order, and trading shells so that everyone has the perfect-sized home!

* Unfortunately, hermit crabs can confuse human trash for shells. They've been seen using bottles, cans, plastic pipes and all sorts of other things. We HAVE to keep our beaches CLEAN!

BFFs and friends from afar are cool...

...but we are ANIMAL ENEMIES!

Some species really have it in for one another. Let us tell you about some of our FIENDISH relationships, some of which are PARASITIC. We eat other species' FOOD, move into their HOMES or even force them to raise our BABIES!

There he goes again, stealing our lunch! We HAVE to stop trusting this guy.

FROGFISH and SMALL SEA CREATURES

Are you all having a dance party?

You know it, Frogfish! Wiggling is kind of our 'thing'.

Can I join in? I know I'm a big fish, but I LOVE the way you all move. It looks like so much fun. Teach me?

Frogfish DON'T dance with small sea creatures... but they DO USE their LURE to imitate their wiggling!

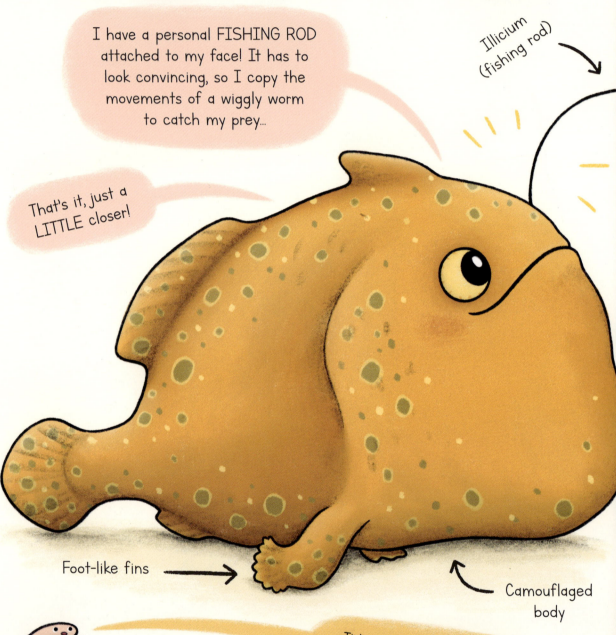

I have a personal FISHING ROD attached to my face! It has to look convincing, so I copy the movements of a wiggly worm to catch my prey...

That's it, just a LITTLE closer!

Illicium (fishing rod)

Foot-like fins

Camouflaged body

I'd rather that fish ate Frogfish's lure than ME!

Agreed. Let's get out of here!

FIND US IN: TROPICAL SEAS, WORLDWIDE

Esca (worm-like lure)

Look at the wiggle on that worm! Sure does look yummy...

Ill-fated little fish

FIENDISH FACTS:

* Sometimes animals use mimicry for SNEAKY reasons. Frogfish use a method of symbiosis called aggressive mimicry to gain an advantage on their prey. It's not parasitic – but it's still pretty MEAN.

* Frogfish actually go fishing! They have a luminescent organ called an esca, which is attached to a long 'rod' called an illicium. They move the esca to make it look like it's a small sea creature. This attracts their prey. The prey mistakes the frogfish's lure as THEIR prey, and when they get too close, they are quickly eaten by the hungry frogfish.

* Frogfish lures come in a number of different shapes, and most of them mimic the look of a sea creature. Some are shaped like a worm, others like a shrimp and there are even frogfish lures that look just like tiny fish – complete with spots for their eyes and appendages that look like fins!

* The rest of the frogfish's body is camouflaged, and because it moves slowly, it looks like a sea sponge or an algae-covered rock. This helps the frogfish to ambush its prey, and also hides it from its own predators. There's just no stopping this sneaky little fish!

Cuckoo birds DON'T ask dunnocks to take care of their eggs... they SNEAK them into their nests! How RUDE.

Then I raise the chick without realising, and the cuckoo doesn't have to parent its young at all!

And it gets WORSE. Not only do I get fed by the overworked dunnock, I even kick the dunnock's tiny chicks out of the nest so I can get the lion's share of the food.

I guess I was just BORN to be SLY!

Worn-out dunnock mother

Super Sneaky!

You were born to be GREEDY!

FIND US IN: WOODLANDS AND GARDENS, EURASIA

FIENDISH FACTS:

*   When a dunnock parent is away from its nest, a cuckoo bird swoops in, removes an egg from the dunnock's nest and replaces it with a cuckoo egg. The dunnock accepts it and raises the chick as its own.

*   The cuckoo egg looks very different from the dunnock egg (it's big and speckled, whereas the dunnock egg is small and blue). However, it is still accepted by the mother dunnock, as she counts the number of eggs rather than paying attention to appearance.

*   Once the cuckoo chick hatches, it pushes the dunnock's eggs or young hatchlings out of the nest to remove competition for food. Nature can be cruel, but this ensures the large cuckoo chick receives enough food from the host dunnock mother for it to survive.

*   Cuckoos have earned this Super Sneaky medallion because they don't just target dunnock birds! They also hide their big speckled eggs in the nests of many other bird species, like pipits and warblers!

*   Cuckoos are so well known for their crafty trick that when other animals do a similar thing in nature, it's known as the 'cuckoo strategy'!

Colossal cuckoo chick

RUBY-THROATED HUMMINGBIRDS and SPIDERS

I'm so beautiful...

...AND clever. Check out this nest I made all by myself!

Everyone just loves me. I'm adorable, I love to eat sugary sweet nectar and I wouldn't hurt a fly!

Sassy fluttering

OK, but like... you've hurt me, Hummingbird. You stole my web!

146

FIND US IN: TROPICAL FORESTS, THE AMERICAS

FIENDISH FACTS:

* Spiders need their webs to catch insects. So the hummingbird destroys both the spider's home AND its food source.

* Hummingbirds steal the webs for making little stretchy nests. The stickiness allows moss and twigs to easily attach, creating a very safe home for their tiny, vulnerable chicks.

* Hummingbirds also benefit by eating any bugs caught in the sticky nests. They sometimes eat the spiders themselves – to add insult to injury!

* Stealing the web can sometimes be dangerous for small hummingbirds, as they can get caught in it – but the benefits usually outweigh the risks.

Stolen spider silk

Stretchy, sticky nest

Drongos DO NOT dress up as meerkats... but they DO **IMITATE** them so that they can **STEAL** their food!

FIENDISH FACTS:

* Drongos earn the trust of a meerkat mob by alerting them when danger (such as a hawk) is nearby. But they break that trust by alerting when there's NO danger around and steal their food as the meerkats run for cover.

* Meerkats get wise to this trick pretty fast, so the drongo tries an even sneakier tactic. It learns the meerkat's special call for danger and repeats it, which tricks the meerkats into thinking a fellow meerkat has seen danger. The drongo then can steal their food to its heart's content!

* Meerkats have extra-sharp claws designed for digging up grubs, and can bite stingers off scorpions to make them easier to eat. This is an added bonus for the drongo, as it couldn't access these snacks itself and they are much more nourishing than the small bugs it would be able to catch on its own.

* Drongo birds have earned a Super Sneaky medallion as they also try this mimic trick with other animals, including weaver birds!

Ahhh!

I can hear the meerkat alarm call!

There must be danger incoming – I'm OUT of here!

Burrow bound meerka

As you can see, there's more to the animal kingdom than meets the eye. There's SO much DRAMA going on behind the scenes!

Our relationships define us – sometimes we get along and at times we really wind each other up.

No matter what types of relationships we share, these connections are important to the health of Earth's ecosystems.

In fact, the one thing we ALL have in common is a BFF relationship with Earth. Look after her, and she'll look after us!

Thanks for living upon me, wonderful creatures!

Humans are really just scratching the surface of how different species interact with each other. We're discovering new ANIMAL BFFs all the time!

Keep your eyes peeled and you might just discover some unlikely animal relationships of your own...

Glossary

Abdomen – another word for an animal's tummy

Aggressive mimicry – a phenomenon in which a predator mimics another animal in order to catch its prey

Agile – an agile animal can move quickly and easily

Antenna – the long, thin parts of an insect's head that it uses to feel with

Aphid – a small bug that feeds by sucking sap from plants

Batesian mimicry – a phenomenon in which a harmless animal mimics a dangerous animal's appearance or behaviour

Camouflage – an animal's colours or patterns that make it difficult for you to see it

Canine – a member of the dog family, which also includes wolves

Carcass – the body of a dead animal

Carnivore – an animal that just eats meat

Carrion – an animal that is already dead (unlike one that another animal has hunted to eat)

Climate – the kind of weather usually found in a certain place. This could be hot or cold, dry or rainy

Commensalism – an animal relationship that benefits one species, and the other species is not affected

Communicate – how animals talk to each other. Sometimes this is by making sounds, but sometimes it is through movements or smells

Coniferous – coniferous trees are evergreen, meaning that they do not shed their leaves in winter. Coniferous forests are found in northern Europe, Asia and North America

Crustacean – a family of animals that includes crabs, lobsters and shrimp

Domestic – related to the home

Dorsal fin – the fin on top of a fish, used for defence and steering

Ecosystem – a community of animals and/or plants in an environment

Evolution – the process by which animals change over time to adapt to their environment

Exoskeleton – a hard skeleton that exists on the outside of some animals' bodies

Feline – a member of the cat family, which also includes lions

Formic acid – a sour, smelly liquid that is found in ant or beetle venom

Groom – how animals clean themselves

Herbivore – an animal that just eats plants

Insect – a family of animals that includes ants, wasps and beetles

Lachryphagy – tear-drinking

Larvae – baby insects

Luminescent – glowing

Lure – a part of an anglerfish's body, that looks like the end of a fishing rod. It tempts smaller fish to swim close so it can eat them. A frogfish is a type of anglerfish

Mammal – a family of animals that includes dogs and people

Metabolism – how an animal's body gets energy from food

Micronutrients – vitamins and minerals that are needed by animals in small amounts

Mimic – copy

Mucus – a type of slime

 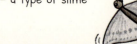

Mutualism – an animal relationship that benefits both species involved

Nectar – a sugary liquid that comes from plants

Nutritious – when a food has lots of goodness in it

Order – a large category of animals

Omnivore – an animal that eats both plants and meat

Parasite – an animal that lives in or on another animal

Parasitism – an animal relationship that benefits one species, at a cost to the other species

Permafrost – ground that remains frozen for at least two years

Pincers – a scorpion's or crab's sharp claws, which open and close

Poacher – a bad person who catches animals illegally

Pollinate – how plants reproduce. When insects feed inside flowers, their legs pick up a sticky powder called pollen. When they move on to the next flower, the pollen brushes off their legs and helps the plant to make new plants

Population – how many of a particular animal live in an area

Prairie – flat, grassy land in Canada or the USA

Predator – an animal that hunts other animals for food

Prey – an animal that is hunted by other animals for food

Savannah – flat, grassy land in Africa

Scavenger – an animal that steals food other animals have hunted, instead of hunting for itself

Solitary – a solitary animal lives alone, rather than in a pack

Species – a kind of animal. A mouse is a different species from a spider, but there are also lots of different kinds of mouse and spider

Subnivean – under snow

Symbiosis – a close relationship between two species, either mutualistic, commensal or parasitic

Tentacle – a flexible limb

Tick – a parasitic, blood-sucking bug

Toxin – another word for poison

Tundra – cold, treeless land, found mostly in the Arctic Circle

Venom – a type of poison that can make you sick if an animal bites or stings you

Wetland – an area of land covered in water, like a marsh

Zooplankton – tiny animals that drift with water currents in fresh or salt water

Further Reading

Want to find out more about the amazing world of animals? Check out these creature feature books!

The (Not) Bad Animals
By Sophie Corrigan
Laugh out loud as you read this book about all the animals around the world that have been given a bad reputation by humans!

The Animal Awards
By Martin Jenkins and Tor Freeman
Celebrate the most spectacular species in the animal kingdom and read all about 50 fantastic creatures that are awarded prizes to celebrate their most dazzling talents and some unusual skills.

What Do Animals Do All Day?
By Wendy Hunt and Studio Muti
What *do* animals do all day? Find out in this fully illustrated book featuring more than 100 animals.

Brimming with creative inspiration, how-to projects, and useful information to enrich your everyday life, Quarto Knows is a favourite destination for those pursuing their interests and passions. Visit our site and dig deeper with our books into your area of interest: Quarto Creates, Quarto Cooks, Quarto Homes, Quarto Lives, Quarto Drives, Quarto Explores, Quarto Gifts, or Quarto Kids.

Animal BFFs © 2022 Quarto Publishing plc. Text and Illustrations © 2022 Sophie Corrigan.

First Published in 2022 by Frances Lincoln Children's Books, an imprint of The Quarto Group.
The Old Brewery, 6 Blundell St, London N7 9BH, United Kingdom.
T (0)20 7700 6700 F (0)20 7700 8066 www.QuartoKnows.com

The right of Sophie Corrigan to be identified as the illustrator and the author of this work has been asserted by her in accordance with the Copyright, Designs and Patents Act, 1988 (United Kingdom).

All rights reserved.

No part of this publication may be reproduced, stored in a retrieval system, or transmitted, in any form, or by any means, electrical, mechanical, photocopying, recording or otherwise without the prior written permission of the publisher or a license permitting restricted copying.

A catalogue record for this book is available from the British Library.

ISBN 978-0-7112-6015-3

The illustrations were created digitally.
Set in DK Crayon Crumble and Letters for Learners

Published by Katie Cotton and Peter Marley
Commissioned by Claire Grace
Designed by Sasha Moxon
Edited by Hattie Grylls
Production by Dawn Cameron

Manufactured in Guangdong China TT122021
9 8 7 6 5 4 3 2 1

77 - 71 = 6

help the   be kind
   poor

1+1=2   love everybody
         be safe

read books be
         positive